AXI

A PARENT'S GUIDE TO FEAR & WORRY

A PARENT'S GUIDE TO

FEAR & WORRY

Tyndale House Publishers
Carol Stream, Illinois

Visit Tyndale online at tyndale.com.

Visit Axis online at axis.org.

Tyndale and Tyndale's quill logo are registered trademarks of Tyndale House Ministries.

A Parent's Guide to Fear & Worry

For information about special discounts for bulk purchases, please contact Tyndale House Publishers at csresponse@tyndale.com, or call 1-855-277-9400.

Library of Congress Cataloging-in-Publication Data

A catalog record for this book is available from the Library of Congress.

ISBN 978-1-4964-6750-8

Printed in the United States of America

29	28	27	26	25	24	23
7	6	5	4	3	2	1

In a way, anxiety is the opposite of fear. Fear is about something that is in front of you that is predictable and imminent. Anxiety is the opposite. It is worrying about something that is in the future that may or may not happen.

CHRISTIAN GRILLON

CONTENTS

A LETTER FROM AXIS

Dear Reader,

We're Axis, and since 2007, we've been creating resources to help connect parents, teens, and Jesus in a disconnected world. We're a group of gospel-minded researchers, speakers, and content creators, and we're excited to bring you the best of what we've learned about making meaningful connections with the teens in your life.

This parent's guide is designed to help start a conversation. Our goal is to give you enough knowledge that you're able to ask your teen informed questions about their world. For each guide, we spend weeks reading, researching, and interviewing parents and teens in order to distill everything you need to know about the topic at hand. We encourage you to read the whole thing and then to use the questions we include to get the conversation going with your teen—and then to follow the conversation wherever it leads.

As Douglas Stone, Bruce Patton, and Sheila Heen point out in their book *Difficult Conversations*, "Changes in attitudes and behavior rarely come about because of arguments, facts, and attempts to persuade. How often do *you* change your values and beliefs—or whom you love or what you want in life—based on something someone tells you? And how likely are you to do so when the person who is trying to change you doesn't seem fully aware of the reasons you see things differently in the first place?"[1] For whatever reason, when we believe that others are trying to understand *our* point of view, our defenses usually go down, and we're more willing to listen to *their* point of view. The rising generation is no exception.

So we encourage you to ask questions, to listen, and then to share your heart with your teen. As we often say at Axis, discipleship happens where conversation happens.

Sincerely,
Your friends at Axis

---

[1] Douglas Stone, Bruce Patton, and Sheila Heen, *Difficult Conversations: How to Discuss What Matters Most*, rev. ed. (New York: Penguin Books, 2010), 137.

"IT'S NOT TIME TO WORRY."

THESE WORDS WERE WRITTEN by Harper Lee in her classic novel *To Kill a Mockingbird*, and they certainly ring true when it comes to our own parental propensity to worry. Will there ever be a convenient time to worry? Hardly! But worry has an ugly way of rearing its head at inconvenient times, as we all know. We try not to worry, but our attempts often seem futile, which in turn makes it hard to be confident in helping our kids navigate through their own fear and worry.

Fear is real—in fact, God created it (more on this below)—but worry is never beneficial. By looking a little closer at the problems of fear and worry, we can learn where they come from, what they are at their root, how to overcome them through the power of God, and how to help our kids do the same.

By looking a little closer
at the problems of fear
and worry, we can learn
where they come from,
what they are at their root,
how to overcome them
through the power of God,
and how to help our kids
do the same.

WHAT IS FEAR?

MERRIAM-WEBSTER defines *fear* as "(n.) an unpleasant often strong emotion caused by anticipation or awareness of danger; anxious concern; (v.) to be afraid of: expect with alarm."[1] Simply put, it's a feeling of alarm that arises in the moment. It can be positive when it warns us of a real danger, such as a car swerving into our lane unexpectedly, or it can be negative when it causes us to anticipate a danger that doesn't exist or has a very unlikely chance of coming to fruition, like that every car within our vicinity is going to swerve into our lane unexpectedly. The first kind of fear causes us to react to something that's actually happening—and can save lives—whereas the second causes us to react to something that *might* happen—and can and *does* steal our peace.

This is important to understand. Because fear is an "unpleasant" emotion, we tend to think of it as being bad in all circumstances—but it's actually not. In fact, as writer Jon Bloom explains:

> Fear is something God designed, not the devil. God designed fear so that we would flee real danger. Fear is meant to be a mercy. Its purpose is to direct us to safety. When our soul is ordered right, we fear the Lord and turn away from evil (Job 28:28). But the devil perverts reality with his lies and seeks to use fear on us backwards. He wants us to fear evil and turn away from the Lord.[2]

"Fear is something God designed, not the devil. God designed fear so that we would flee real danger. Fear is meant to be a mercy. Its purpose is to direct us to safety."

—JON BLOOM

This means it's important for us to discern between healthy and unhealthy fear— so we can reject the devil's attempts at distracting us and keeping us from the abundant life God has planned for us.[3]

We will always face temptations to fear, so we need to be ready to face it. If we don't, fear quickly transforms into worry.

WHAT IS WORRY?

YOU MAY HAVE HEARD THIS QUOTE, attributed to Mark Twain: "I am an old man and have known a great many troubles, but most of them have never happened."[4] We parents have lived long enough to recognize the wisdom of this statement. It's easy to anticipate bad things happening, but many times those troubles never come.

Oxford Dictionary defines *worry* as "(n.) The state of being anxious and troubled over actual or potential problems; (v.) Feel or cause to feel anxious or troubled about actual or potential problems."[5] Worry is the act of meditating on the things we're fearful about and, in a sense, it actually distracts us from facing our fears. It causes us to obsess over a fear and stay mentally trapped, rather than acknowledge the fear and work to move past it.

Psychotherapist Katherine Schafler offers this definition of worrying and how it relates to fear:

> Worrying pretends to be necessary, but it's not proactive and it's not helpful. Worrying buddies up with your imagination to exploit your fears. Worrying is focusing your thoughts on all the negative outcomes at the opportunity cost of applying that same energy towards problem solving. Fears need a combination of acceptance and positive reassurance to be managed.[6]

While worry focuses on a negative expectation, causing fear to be magnified, fear happens more suddenly and is generally unexpected. Worry is generally thought

"Worry does not empty tomorrow of its sorrow, it empties today of its strength."

–CORRIE TEN BOOM

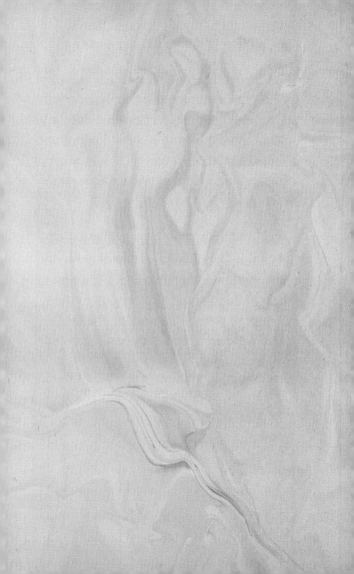

of as being ongoing, while fear is more spontaneous, something that happens in the moment. Fear is a more momentary type of alarm; worry is what keeps fear going. Fear sparks worry, while worry rehearses fears from every possible angle, allowing the fear to linger.

In her book *Clippings from My Notebook*, Corrie ten Boom wrote, "Worry does not empty tomorrow of its sorrow, it empties today of its strength."[7] Worry takes away our energy to face life and its challenges. When we give in to worry, we allow fear to rule our lives.

HOW ARE FEAR AND WORRY RELATED TO ANXIETY?

DEPENDING ON ONE'S CIRCUMSTANCES, as the *New York Times Magazine* explains, anxiety can be "a rational reaction to unstable, dangerous circumstances." This is similar to what we identified earlier as a healthy type of fear. However, when anxiety takes hold of a person, it wreaks havoc in their mind, similar to worry: "Highly anxious people . . . have an overactive fight-or-flight response that perceives threats where there often are none."[8] In her book *On Edge: A Journey through Anxiety*, Andrea Petersen writes, "Anxious people aren't just constantly on guard; they actually see more peril in the world." She follows this up a few pages later by quoting Christian Grillon, who observes: "In a way, anxiety is the opposite of fear. Fear is about something that is in front of you that is predictable and imminent. Anxiety is the opposite. It is worrying about something that is in the future that may or may not happen."[9]

While most people experience some degree of anxiety surrounding the circumstances of their lives, more severe anxiety struggles require professional medical attention to be managed and overcome. Anxiety is a mental health disorder, the diagnosis of which is becoming increasingly common in Generation Z. In fact, it has overtaken depression as the most common reason college students seek out counseling.[10]

"Fear is about something that is in front of you that is predictable and imminent. Anxiety is the opposite. It is worrying about something that is in the future that may or may not happen."

—CHRISTIAN GRILLON

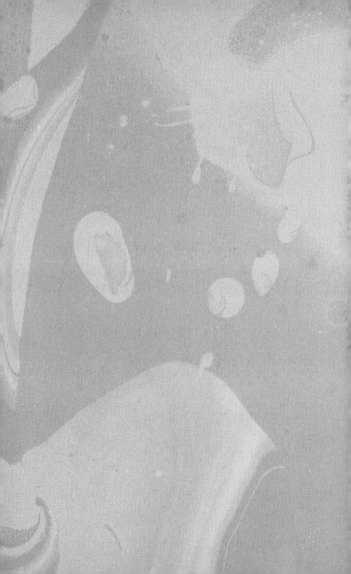

HOW DOES CULTURE PLAY INTO OUR FEARS?

AS BELIEVERS, WE BELONG TO CHRIST, but as John points out in his first epistle, "the whole world lies in the power of the evil one."[11] We see every day how culture creates, perpetuates, and even exploits many of our fears. Mainstream media tends to focus on negative or frightening events—of which there is no shortage—many times exaggerating them to seem like a larger source of fear than they are. News items covering social justice issues, violence, and political topics can all be points of contention and, if we're not careful, sources of fear and worry. Even the music, movies, and TV we consume can cause us to worry about whether we're hustling enough or good enough or rich enough or beautiful enough or *anything* enough. And many companies use our existing fears or create new ones in order to sell their products (e.g., almost every "beauty" product ever created).

Another source of fear that's unique to the twenty-first century and immensely powerful is social media. Regardless of the original goal of different platforms, most (if not all) have devolved into major sources of anxiety, fear, insecurity, and worry. Of course, there are exceptions, but for most users, it's too easy to compare ourselves to what others are posting, feel like we don't measure up, then post something that makes us look better, which in turn is seen by others who don't feel like they measure up, and on the cycle goes.[12] This is something that impacts teenagers immensely. Forty-five percent said they feel judged on social platforms (fear of other people's opinions or FOPO), and 38 percent reported feeling bad about themselves due to their use of social media (fear of not being good enough).[13]

WHAT FEARS ARE COMMON FOR GEN Z?

BASED ON STEREOTYPES—e.g., "the selfie generation"—it would be reasonable to expect Gen Zers' greatest fears to be self-focused, but when we look at generation-specific statistics from studies in both the USA[14] and the UK,[15] it's clear that their worries are much more outwardly focused. Societal issues at large are significant sources of fear for them, and this can largely be attributed to the use of social media as a tool to get information about and discuss current social issues. In a sense, the young adults of Generation Z (born mid- to late-1990s to mid-2010s) are more grounded in reality, so they may feel they have more reason to fear.

According to these studies, Gen Z's greatest fears are

- Terrorism
- School safety

- Gun violence

- The state of the government

- Debt and lack of ability to find work

These outward-facing fears have extremely inward-facing consequences, as we touched on earlier. Gen Z is highly anxious in general. They have a greater struggle with mental health issues and are stressed about rising suicide rates. In a CNN article on Gen Z, Andrea Diaz reported, "Although 62% of Generation Z said rising suicide rates are also a source of stress, compared with 44% of adults overall, the survey says these young people are more likely to report mental health conditions than any other generation."[16] Though this may sound grim, it can also be viewed in a more positive light, indicating that this generation truly cares about their mental health and is

[Gen Z] people are more likely to report mental health conditions than any other generation . . . indicating that this generation truly cares about their mental health and is self-aware enough to know when they need help.

self-aware enough to know when they need help.

The story of Jake is one that's all too common for young millennials (born late 1980s to mid-1990s) and Gen Zers. He was a young man who battled severe anxiety with no one specific thing that seemed to have caused it. Instead, it was a pileup of multiple Advanced Placement classes and extracurriculars he felt he had to juggle in order to ensure admission into a good college so he could ultimately have a great career. His anxiety essentially paralyzed him to the point that he believed if he failed a single quiz at school, "Then I'll get a bad grade in the class, I won't get into the college I want, I won't get a good job and I'll be a total failure." Thankfully, he was able to get intensive therapy and move on in life with his anxiety under control—and he even got into his dream university.[17]

WHY DO THEY HAVE SO MUCH FEAR AND WORRY?

THOUGH THERE'S NOTHING NEW under the sun,[18] each generation has struggles that are different from those of previous generations. For Gen Z, culture consistently tells them, "You are in charge of your own destiny. It's all up to you." While personal responsibility is important, the pressure of controlling one's own destiny is too much weight to bear. At the root of ungodly fear and worry is a desire to control and a belief that each of us has total responsibility for our own destiny. This is a version of pride because, by attempting to control everything in our lives, we develop the mindset of thinking we have a better handle on things than God and that He will not help us. Pride places us on the throne of our own hearts and also makes us feel like the weight of our fears and worries is ours alone to carry. Ultimately, however, if we surrender to God, His purpose will prevail. Proverbs

19:21 reminds us, "Many are the plans in a person's heart, but it is the LORD's purpose that prevails."

In addition, fear of man (worrying about what others think of us more than what God does) is something that all people of all generations struggle with, but Gen Z is living in a time when this fear is on steroids. Just like other fears, it's prideful because it's another way we attempt to control our own lives. Pastor John Piper wrote, "Fear of men really is a mark of pride. It is presumptuous. It presumes to take over a responsibility for our comfort which God has said *he* wants to handle. . . . So fear takes over the role of protector and guide and comforter."[19] Fear of man attempts to control how others view us at the expense of keeping God at the forefront of our hearts, decisions, and actions.

WHAT DOES SCRIPTURE SAY?

THROUGHOUT SCRIPTURE, God consistently commands his people not to fear or worry. Instead, we are to trust Him in all things. In fact, one writer points out that the phrase "do not be afraid" is found in the NIV **seventy times** and, "more often than not, is followed by an action that God is or will be taking."[20] These actions include promises such as deliverance, victory, and protection.

God commands Abraham not to fear in Genesis 15:1, when He says, "Do not be afraid, Abram. I am your shield, your very great reward." Then in Genesis 46:3, God assures Moses, "I am God, the God of your father. . . . Do not be afraid to go down to Egypt, for I will make you into a great nation there." In the New Testament, Jesus tells His disciples, "Do not be afraid, little flock, for your Father has been pleased to give you the kingdom" (Luke 12:32). In the book of Revelation, the apostle John reacts in fear to his vision of Jesus, to which Jesus replies, "Do not be afraid. I am the First and the Last. I am the Living One; I was dead, and now look, I am alive for ever and ever! And I hold the keys of death and Hades" (Revelation 1:17-18).

These and many other examples remind us that we can release our fears, worries, and need to be in control because the Lord is fighting on our behalf. We live our lives for the sake of Christ because He already gave Himself up for us (see Galatians 2:20). He Himself is our reward (see Genesis 15:1). He delights to share His Kingdom with us. He has been present since before the beginning of time, and He has conquered death. When Jesus returns, He will wipe away all of our tears (see Isaiah 25:8). And above all, He is sovereign over all things (see Isaiah

The phrase "do not be afraid" is found in the NIV seventy times and, "more often than not, is followed by an action that God is or will be taking."

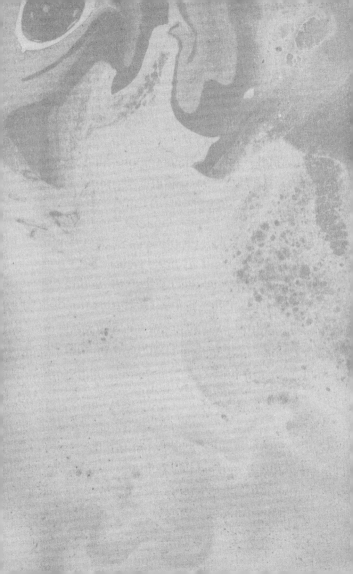

55:9, Lamentations 3:37-38, Daniel 4:17, Matthew 10:29, John 19:10-11, Hebrews 1:3, Colossians 1:17).

Even though we have the promise of care from the Lord and, ultimately, eternal justice, we have to keep in mind that we are currently in a battle against the forces of darkness. *Satan would love nothing more than to prevent us from victory over fear.* His ultimate goal is to destroy us and our faith. In 1 Peter 5:8-9, he is described as a "roaring lion looking for someone to devour," but he often devours us in subtle and deceptive ways. Rather than risk being detected by being too forthright and obvious, the enemy seeks to lull us into a place of stagnancy or distraction. When we're concerned about the things of the world, we don't view them through the lens of God's final victory and our place in His Kingdom.

In C. S. Lewis's book *The Screwtape Letters*, he writes from the perspective of a senior demon training a junior demon on how to prevent Christians from keeping the faith and being productive members of the Kingdom of God. (Since it's written as a satire, in the following excerpt the word "Enemy" is used to refer to God.) Lewis writes, "There is nothing like suspense and anxiety for barricading a human's mind against the Enemy. He wants men to be concerned with what they do; our business is to keep them thinking about what will happen to them."[21] Satan wants desperately to pit believers against Christ within their hearts and minds by distracting us with fears, anxieties, insecurities, discouragement, and worry.

In addition to what we mentioned above, the Bible tells us many other things about fear and worry:

- Because we have been adopted as children of God, we no longer have to remain in bondage to fear (Romans 8:15; 1 John 4:18).

- The fear of man traps us, but trusting in the Lord keeps us safe (Psalm 56:3-4; Proverbs 29:25).

- Jesus said we should not be anxious about our lives or worry about tomorrow, but should be focused on how God meets our needs today. We do not need to be anxious about whether He will provide for us (Matthew 6:25-34; Luke 12:22-24).

- There is no need to fear because God is on our side (Psalm 118:6).

- We can be encouraged because God is on His way to save His people (Isaiah 35:4).

- When horrible, fear-inducing things happen around us, we can have confident faith because "he who is in you is greater than he who is in the world" (1 John 4:4, ESV).

- We are instructed not to be anxious but to make our requests known to God. When we do so, He will guard us with his peace (Philippians 4:6-7).

There will always be things we could fear, especially when it comes to raising our kids, but we can have courage and faith that God will help us through every question and struggle. We can seek to release our burdens to the Lord, and as Jesus said, "find rest for your souls" (Matthew 11:28-30). Jesus promised peace for us through the coming of the Holy Spirit: "Peace I leave with you; my peace I give to you. Not as the world gives do I give to you. Let not your hearts be troubled, neither let them be afraid" (John 14:27, ESV). Through the power of the Holy Spirit, peace—rather than fear—can rule our hearts. Isaiah 41:10 (ESV) says, "Fear not, for I am with you; be not dismayed, for I am your God; I will strengthen you, I will help you, I will uphold you with my righteous right hand." When we experience fear, we can choose to release it to God and take on His strength instead.

HOW DO I RESIST A SPIRIT OF FEAR?

PAUL ENCOURAGED TIMOTHY, "God has not given us a spirit of fear, but of power and of love and of a sound mind."[22] But tapping into that power and love requires discipline and active participation on our part. We must cultivate this habit daily, possibly even minute by minute.

First, we must release control and be humble before God, acknowledging Him as the source of all we need. When we do this, we can freely cast our anxieties on Christ, trusting with confidence that He cares for us.[23] This requires that we acknowledge our fears and worries rather than stuffing them away or pretending they don't exist or matter. It also requires that we take God at His word and trust that He will do what He says, even when it seems impossible. This means we step out in faith and do as God asks, regardless of what He has or has not done yet. Piper describes this correlation between fear and obedience: "God promises to be our comforter and protector, but [if we live in fear] we deny the credibility of God's word and allow fear to set the limits of our obedience"—i.e. "I'll do that *after* God does this."[24]

As children of God, when we're tempted to succumb to fear and worry, we should instead turn our focus back to God through praise and prayer. Listen to praise and worship music. Pray with a friend. Post encouraging Scriptures around your home where they can be easily seen. Do whatever it takes to meditate on God's Word instead of your worry. Focus on God's promises. Don't pretend that fear doesn't exist in your life, but also don't let it linger and have free reign. If you let your fear control you and dictate your decisions, you're setting that example for your children when they encounter their own fears.

Listen to praise and worship music. Pray with a friend. Post encouraging Scriptures around your home where they can be easily seen. Do whatever it takes to meditate on God's Word instead of your worry.

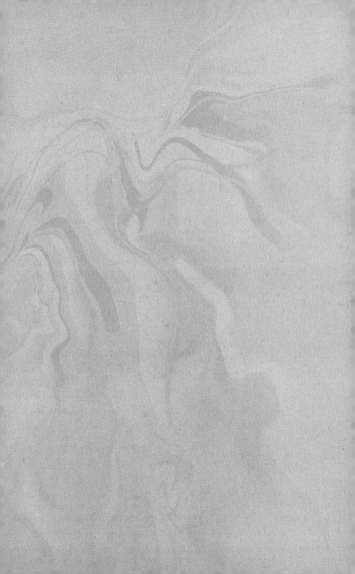

HOW DO I HELP MY KIDS DO THE SAME?

AS WE JUST MENTIONED, the best way to disciple your kids into having a biblical perspective of fear and worry is to model it by how you live. Seek the Lord and His Word for wisdom; take a class at your church; get professional counseling assistance—do whatever it takes. In doing so, you'll be better equipped to help your kids. Proverbs 14:26 says, "Whoever fears the LORD has a secure fortress, and for their children it will be a refuge." When you keep God as the supreme authority in your life, not only does it make you secure, but it brings stability to your children as well.

Second, allow your children to acknowledge their fear and worry—there is no shame in having those feelings, but it's not healthy to stay in that headspace long-term. When we bring our fear into the light, it loses its power (see Ephesians

5:13). Think of ways to make your home a safe place to talk about fear and worry, no matter how shameful they might seem. Be the one to bring up the topic first; if you don't talk about a subject, your kids will learn implicitly that it's off limits. So share about your own fears (especially triumphs over them!) and ask your kids about theirs. Remind them that they are safe with you and they will not be judged.

Don't let the conversation end there. Talk to your kids about how, by God's power and grace, they can overcome their anxieties and worries. Train them to live in the fear of the Lord, not the fear of man. Teach them about the peace that comes from the Holy Spirit's presence in their lives. Teach them to seek the Lord and listen for His voice. Disciple them in what it means to be content (see Hebrews 13:5-6). Teach them to seek the Lord for consolation in their struggles: "When the cares of my heart are many, your consolations cheer my soul" (Psalm 94:19, ESV). By discipling your children in the ways of the Lord, you are together building a solid spiritual foundation that will help them hold fast to God in every circumstance.

By discipling your children
in the ways of the Lord, you
are together building a solid
spiritual foundation that
will help them hold fast to
God in every circumstance.

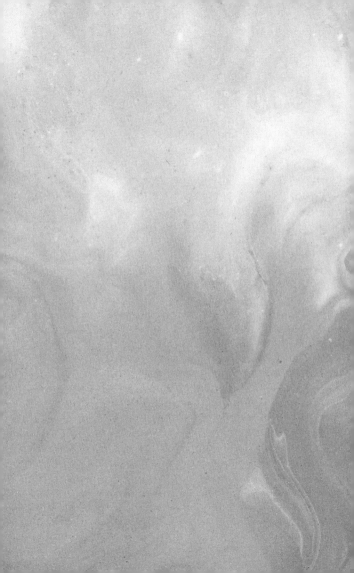

HOW DO I HELP A CHILD WHO STRUGGLES WITH FEAR AND WORRY?

SEEING A CHILD STRUGGLE in this area can make us want to control the situation. Controlling behavior doesn't help, though. In her book *On Edge*, Andrea Petersen talks about how detrimental controlling behavior can be when it comes to helping our children with fear and anxiety issues: "Overprotective and controlling parenting—telling kids what to think and feel and micromanaging their activities— sends the message that children aren't capable, a belief that can fuel anxiety."[25]

Don't beat yourself up if you have a child who struggles in this area. Petersen also points out that "researchers found that parenting explained only about 4 percent of the variation in anxiety issues among children."[26] Get your child professional help if needed. Therapy and counseling are wonderful tools that God can work through.

Encourage your child to find Bible passages or quotations that they can put up in their room or carry with them in their backpack when they are tempted to worry. "Anxious hearts are very heavy, but a word of encouragement does wonders!" (Proverbs 12:25, TLB). Offer to help find some verses with them. A great verse to meditate on is Psalm 34:4: "I sought the LORD, and he answered me; he delivered me from all my fears." Help your child find activities to do when they are worried, things that will send their mental energy in a more positive direction. Some people find a lot of peace in volunteering to help others. Others enjoy exercising, cooking, or playing a musical instrument. Finally, never underestimate the power of God's Word and the power of praying for your children (see Romans 12:12).

Help your child find
activities to do when
they are worried, things
that will send their
mental energy in a
more positive direction.

RECAP

- While not all fear is bad, it is not meant to stay for long. Fear that is allowed to linger transitions to worry.

- Fear can be a protective impulse; it gets off base when it is allowed to turn into worry and rule in a person's mind.

- Negative news stories and the pressures associated with social media contribute to the increasing number of Generation Zers who suffer from anxiety disorder and fears related to society at large.

- Feelings of fear and worry are natural, but as children of God, we are free to release fear and walk in His peace instead.

- Pride or a desire to control are often at the root of our fear and worry issues.

- As parents, we need to humble ourselves before God so we may release our own fear and worry to Him and walk in obedience. In doing so, we will set a godly example for our children and be prepared to disciple them.

- God is ultimately the One in control, so we can give Him the pressure we feel to control our lives and our children's lives.

DISCUSSION
QUESTIONS

1. How often do you worry or feel afraid?

2. What are some of the things you're afraid of?

3. What do you do when you're afraid or anxious? Does it help?

4. How can I help you when you're feeling that way?

5. Do you feel like God helps you with your fears and worries? Why or why not?

6. Have you ever felt afraid to talk about something that scares you? Why or why not?

7. Are there things you do that could contribute to your anxiety and worry? If so, what are they? How can I help you not to do those things?

8. Why do you think God tells us not to be afraid so much in the Bible?

9. Do you ever feel like you're the only one who struggles with a certain fear or worry? Why or why not?

10. What does it look like to "cast your cares on God"? Is that easy or hard to do?

11. Are there new habits that would help you focus on God's promises rather than on your fears? How can I help you with those?

CONCLUSION

THERE IS NO SHORTAGE of things to fear in our world. Each day there's a new story of hardship and suffering that could lead us to worry about our children's lives and experiences. The good news is that, in Christ, we have an open invitation to relinquish our fear and worry and replace them with His peace. Fear and worry do not have to control your life or your kids' lives. Jesus never guaranteed us a hardship-free life, but He has made provision for our peace in the midst of life's storms: "I have said these things to you, that in me you may have peace. In the world you will have tribulation. But take heart; I have overcome the world" (John 16:33, ESV).

Fear and worry do not have to control your life or your kids' lives. Jesus never guaranteed us a hardship-free life, but He has made provision for our peace in the midst of life's storms.

ADDITIONAL
RESOURCES

1. "Stress in America: Generation Z," 2018 Report, American Psychological Association, https://www.apa.org/news/press/releases/stress/2018/stress-gen-z.pdf

2. *Emotionally Healthy Spirituality* by Peter Scazzero

NOTES

1. "Fear (n.) and (v.)," Merriam-Webster, accessed June 1, 2022, https://www.merriam-webster.com/dictionary/fear.

2. Jon Bloom, "Lay Aside the Weight of Fear," Desiring God, April 19, 2013, https://www.desiringgod.org/articles/lay-aside-the-weight-of-fear.

3. See Ephesians 6:10-18.

4. "Worry Quotes," Goodreads, accessed June 1, 2022, https://www.goodreads.com/quotes/tag/worry?page=2.

5. "Worry (v.)," Lexico, accessed June 1, 2022, https://www.lexico.com/definition/worry.

6. Katherine Schafler, "The Big Difference between Fear and Worry," Shine, December 5, 2017, https://advice.theshineapp.com/articles/the-difference-between-fear-worry/.

7. Corrie ten Boom, *Clippings from My Notebook* (Thorndike, ME: Thorndike Press, 1983), 43.

8. Benoit Denizet-Lewis, "Why Are More American Teenagers Than Ever Suffering from Severe Anxiety?" *New York Times Magazine*, October 11, 2017, https://www.nytimes.com /2017/10/11/magazine/why-are-more -american-teenagers-than-ever-suffering -from-severe-anxiety.html.

9. Andrea Petersen, *On Edge: A Journey through Anxiety* (New York: Crown, 2017), 31, 34.

10. Emily Tate, "Anxiety on the Rise," Inside Higher Ed, March 29, 2017, https://www .insidehighered.com/news/2017/03/29/anxiety -and-depression-are-primary-concerns -students-seeking-counseling-services.

11. 1 John 5:19, ESV

12. "Are You Living an Insta Lie? Social Media vs. Reality," Ditch the Label, YouTube, video, 3:12, February 20, 2017, https://www.youtube.com /watch?v=0EFHbruKEmw.

13. Andrea Diaz, "Generation Z Reported the Most Mental Health Problems, and Gun Violence Is the Biggest Stressor," CNN, October 30, 2018, https://www.cnn.com/2018/10/30/health /generation-z-stress-report-trnd/index.html.

14. Diaz, "Generation Z Reported the Most Mental Health Problems."

15. Jessica Stillman, "Gen Z Is Anxious, Distrustful, and Often Downright Miserable, New Poll Reveals," Inc., accessed June 1, 2022, https://www.inc.com/jessica-stillman/gen-z-is-anxious-distrustful-and-often-downright-miserable-new-poll-reveals.html.

16. Diaz, "Generation Z Reported the Most Mental Health Problems."

17. Denizet-Lewis, "Why Are More American Teenagers Than Ever Suffering from Severe Anxiety?"

18. See Ecclesiastes 1:9.

19. John Piper, "The Pride of Being Afraid," Desiring God, May 19, 1981, https://www.desiringgod.org/articles/the-pride-of-being-afraid.

20. "The Most Frequent Command in the Bible," Body Tithe University, accessed June 1, 2022, https://bodytithe.com/frequent-command-bible/.

21. C. S. Lewis, *The Screwtape Letters* (New York: HarperOne, 2001), 25.

22. 2 Timothy 1:7, NKJV

23. See 1 Peter 5:6-7.

24. Piper, "The Pride of Being Afraid."

25. Petersen, *On Edge*, 47.

26. Petersen, *On Edge*, 48.

PARENT GUIDES TO FINDING TRUE IDENTITY
BY AXIS

When culture is constantly pulling teens away from Christian values, let these five parent guides spark an ongoing conversation about finding your true identity in Christ.

BUNDLE THESE 5 BOOKS AND SAVE

DISCOVER MORE PARENT GUIDES, VIDEOS, AND AUDIOS AT AXIS.ORG

www.axis.org

CP1814